# HAND, HAND, FINGERS, THUMB

BY AL PERKINS

ILLUSTRATED BY ERIC GURNEY

COLLINS

Trademark of Random House, Inc., William Collins Sons & Co. Ltd., Authorised User

6 7 8 9 10

ISBN 0 00 171270 5 (paperback)
ISBN 0 00 171205 5 (hardback)

Copyright © 1969 by Random House, Inc.
A Bright and Early Book for Beginning Beginners
published by arrangement with
Random House Inc., New York, New York
First published in Great Britain 1970

Printed & bound in Hong Kong

Hand
Hand

Fingers

Thumb

One thumb
One thumb
Drumming on a drum.

One hand
Two hands
Drumming on a drum.

Dum ditty
Dum ditty
Dum dum dum.

# Rings on fingers.

# Rings on thumb.

Drum drum
Drum drum
Drum drum drum.

Monkeys drum . . .

. . . and monkeys hum.

Hum drum
Hum drum
Hum drum hum.

Hand picks an apple.

Hand picks a plum.

Dum ditty
Dum ditty
Dum dum dum.

Monkeys come
And monkeys go.

Hands with handkerchiefs.
Blow! Blow! Blow!

"Hello Jack."

"Hello Jake."

Shake hands
Shake hands
Shake! Shake! Shake!

## "Bye-bye Jake."

## "Bye-bye Jack."

Dum ditty
Dum ditty

Whack! Whack! Whack!

Hands play banjos
Strum strum strum.

# Hands play fiddles
## Zum zum zum.

Dum ditty
Dum ditty
Dum dum dum,

# Hand in hand
## More monkeys come.

Many more fingers.
Many more thumbs.
Many more monkeys.
Many more drums.

Millions of fingers!
Millions of thumbs!
Millions of monkeys
Drumming on drums!

Dum

ditty

Dum

ditty

Dum

dum

dum.